THE RISE AND FALL OF THE BYZANTINE EMPIRE

MONIQUE VESCIA

ROSEN
PUBLISHING

To my beloved father, Fernando Vescia (1929–2014), who knew his way around Byzantium long before I arrived.

Published in 2017 by The Rosen Publishing Group, Inc.
29 East 21st Street, New York, NY 10010

First Edition

Library of Congress Cataloging-in-Publication Data

Names: Vescia, Monique, author.
Title: The rise and fall of the Byzantine Empire / Monique Vescia.
Description: First edition. | New York : Rosen Publishing, 2017. | Series:
  The rise and fall of empires | Includes bibliographical references and
  index. | Audience: Grade 7 to 12._
Identifiers: LCCN 2015048428| ISBN 9781499463361 (library bound) |
ISBN
  9781499463347 (pbk.) | ISBN 9781499463354 (6-pack)
Subjects: LCSH: Byzantine Empire—History.
Classification: LCC DF504.5 .V47 2016 | DDC 949.5/02—dc23
LC record available at http://lccn.loc.gov/2015048428

Manufactured in China

CONTENTS

INTRODUCTION

People often refer to the fall of the mighty Roman Empire in 476 CE, but that date is nearly a millennium premature. What we now call the Byzantine Empire was actually a continuation of the Roman Empire, founded upon the new religion of Christianity and centered in Constantinople (later renamed Istanbul), in present-day Turkey. This brilliant and cosmopolitan civilization would repel many enemy assaults and endure for another thousand years before finally falling to the Ottoman Turks in 1453.

The Mediterranean, from the Latin meaning "middle land," was central to the expansion and ultimate destiny of the Roman Empire as its power center shifted from west to east.

Byzantium, as the empire came to be called, was Greek-speaking and had a distinctly eastern character. At its height, Byzantium impressed both its allies and its many enemies with its lavish displays of wealth, the sophistication of its culture, and its religious art and architecture. The capital city of Constantinople attracted travelers from everywhere, becoming a thriving hub of international trade. Far more than their western Roman counterparts, the Byzantines were curious about other cultures and open to new ideas. While much of western Europe remained illiterate, the Byzantines nurtured scholarship in their schools and monasteries. Women had access to education and often wielded a remarkable degree of power and influence.

Today, many scholars believe that the Byzantine Empire made western civilization possible. Byzantine scholarly traditions helped preserve classical Greek and Latin texts, which would otherwise have been lost or destroyed. By checking the spread of Islam into the west, the Byzantines gave western Europe time to develop its own cultures and traditions and to experience a rebirth, known as the Renaissance. We would live in a very different world today if the Byzantine Empire had never existed.

CHAPTER 1

THE NEW ROME: ORIGINS OF THE BYZANTINE EMPIRE

In 117 CE, the Roman Empire reached the height of its power. Imperial Rome's unrivalled military strength and its belief in its own superiority had enabled it to seize territory as far north and west as Britain and western Europe (modern Italy, France, Spain, Greece, and Turkey) and south and east into northern Africa, Arabia, and Asia Minor. Roman forces brutally subdued the inhabitants of these lands and plundered their resources to enrich the empire. They also imposed order and stability, establishing postal systems, building fine roads, and erecting stone aqueducts to channel water into the cities that rose up along these routes.

A DIVIDED EMPIRE

As a result of this unchecked expansion, the Roman Empire was overstretched. With so many frontiers to defend, it had to constantly fight expensive wars. Taxing Roman citizens to pay for military spending had widened the gap between the rich and the poor, stirring anger in the populace. By the middle of the third century CE, the once glorious capital of Rome had suffered a serious decline. Leaders were often corrupt and changed frequently at the whims of the army. The city was in chaos, threatened by barbarian enemies. Sickness, hunger, and fear shadowed the streets of the capital.

A military general brought to power by his legion in 284 CE, the emperor Diocletian understood that the Roman Empire had grown too large to be governed by a single person. Diocletian developed a system of co-rulers to reign over an empire divided into eastern and western halves.

THE RISE OF CONSTANTINE

Constantius was a brilliant general who became one of the four rulers of the Roman Empire. When he died in Britain in 306, the army named his son, Constantine, as his successor. The new emperor did not believe in sharing

Before an important battle, Constantine supposedly had a vision that prompted his conversion to Christianity: he saw a cross above the sun, with the words *Conquer by this* engraved upon it.

power, and over the next eighteen years he managed to engage his three co-rulers in battle and eliminate them. To consolidate his power, Constantine also had his sons and his wife put to death, as well as many of his political rivals.

By 324, Constantine had become the sole ruler of the Roman Empire. Sometimes referred to as Constantine the Great, he would become one of the most influential rulers in history. Within a fifteen-year span, Constantine made two decisions that would change course of the world: he adopted Christianity as the religion of the Roman Empire, and he moved the empire's capital from Rome to the east, to the site of a former Greek trading colony.

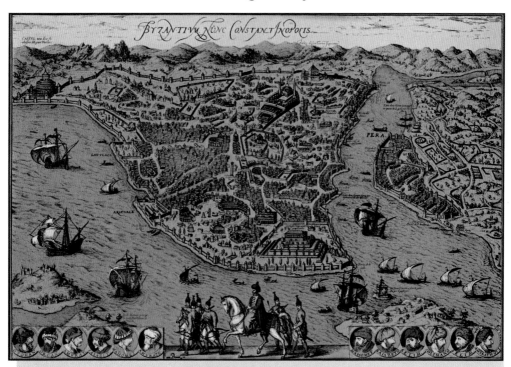

Constantine picked an excellent spot to build his city. This map (made after the Turkish conquest) offers a bird's-eye view of the many water routes around the peninsula.

LOCATION, LOCATION, LOCATION

The site that Constantine chose for the eastern capital of the Roman Empire sits at the tip of an elevated peninsula of land between the inland Sea of Marmara and the Black Sea, in what is present-day Turkey. The original city, a trading colony called Byzantium by the Greeks who founded it a thousand years before, was not large or famous, but it was strategically important. The settlement was positioned at a major intersection of trade routes between the East and the West. At the narrowest point of the Bosporus Strait, the continents of Europe and Asia are just 700 yards apart. To the south, from the Sea of Marmara, ships can sail out to the Mediterranean and from there to Greece, western Europe, Africa, and beyond. The rough currents of the Bosporus made attacking Constantinople difficult from the sea. To the north of the city, an estuary known as the Golden Horn provided a deep and well-protected harbor for ships. The people who built the nearby city of Chalcedon became legendary for their blindness, because they had been oblivious to the presence of a far superior location just opposite the strait from their settlement.

ROME REBORN

In the eastern provinces, Constantine saw an opportunity to restore the Roman Empire's former glory. Western territories had been plundered to fund the empire's imperial ambitions and further ravaged by Rome's enemies. The Greek-speaking lands to the east had long been more prosperous and cultured than those in the west. In

Byzantium, Constantine planned to establish a shining new capital, a "nova roma" or New Rome. The city, which required vast resources and many years to build, became known as Constantinople, meaning Constantine's City.

Constantine wanted the city named after him to be the most beautiful one on Earth. He looted the western cities, carrying away their finest works of art to beautify and enrich the new Roman capital on the Bosporus. He also ordered a wall to be built to protect the city from invaders. In 330, Constantinople was formally named the seat of the Roman Empire.

Today, people refer to the territories ruled from Constantinople as the Byzantine Empire. The government and culture that originated from this center is known as Byzantium. However, the people we call the Byzantines would have been puzzled by that word. They considered themselves Romans.

THE COUNCIL OF NICAEA

Over time, Constantinople's inhabitants slowly abandoned their pagan beliefs, and adopted the new faith their emperor had chosen.

As the Christian faith gained followers, people often vigorously—and sometimes violently—debated specific religious questions. Church leaders believed that a shared system of beliefs would help avoid conflict and unify believers within the faith. A series of meetings, called ecumenical councils, were held to try to iron out disagreements.

THE RISE OF CHRISTIANITY

The world's most populous religion, with an estimated 2.2 billion adherents worldwide in 2010, began as an obscure Jewish sect.

Until the fourth century, the official Roman religion was polytheistic: like the ancient Greeks, the Romans worshiped many gods and goddesses, such as Mars (the god of war), and Venus (the goddess of love). Most of the time, the Romans tolerated other religious beliefs, allowing other religious sects to practice within Roman society. As long as people submitted to the authority of the state and did not stir up trouble, they could worship as they pleased.

Around 30 CE, Jews in the Roman Empire began following the teachings of a man called Jesus of Nazareth. Word spread that Christ spoke of a heavenly kingdom, greater than Rome. This new inclusive faith attracted increasing numbers of believers, especially among ordinary people and the poor. The Roman emperors perceived it as a threat and began to persecute its followers in an attempt to suppress it. The crucifixion of Jesus only served to fuel the spread of Christianity.

The new religion got another boost when the emperor Constantine embraced Christianity. It became the official faith of the Roman Empire in 391 CE during the reign of Theodosius I.

Christian belief in one god helped support the idea of a single ruler on Earth. Its widespread appeal would serve to unify a fractured empire.

A Russian fresco depicting the first Council of Nicaea, presided over by Constantine. The emperor holds a royal scepter in one hand and the planet Earth in the other.

The first of these meetings, held in 325 in the city of Nicaea, was organized by Constantine himself. Among other issues, he wanted to settle the question of Christ's relationship to God. What was the nature of Jesus Christ? Was he human or divine, or some combination of the two? After much discussion, the Council came up with the concept of the Trinity: a unity of three, comprised of God the father, the Son, and the Holy Spirit. The meeting resulted in the church adopting the Nicene Creed, a summary of the main ideas of Christian belief. The Creed is still recited at Catholic masses today, nearly seventeen centuries later.

CHAPTER 2

BIRTH OF A SUPERPOWER: THE EARLY BYZANTINE PERIOD (330–842)

In its first century, Constantinople rapidly exceeded the city limits that Constantine had established in 330. In seventy years the population increased tenfold, from 30,000 to 300,000. The emperor Theodosius II (reigned 408–50) further fortified the city when he had a ring of double walls and a moat constructed to help keep out invaders approaching from the west. The mighty Theodosian Walls, constructed of alternating layers of stone and brick, repelled attackers for more than a thousand years.

A FORTIFIED CAPITAL

By the seventh century, the Byzantines had devised a defensive weapon that terrified enemies that tried to attack the city by water. Known as "Greek fire," its exact ingredients were a closely guarded secret. Defenders sprayed this petroleum-based liquid at attacking ships, setting them ablaze. Historical accounts describe flames spewing from the mouths of metal lions mounted on Byzantine warships.

13

The exact formula has been lost, but Greek fire may have consisted of petroleum, quicklime, and sulfur. The compound acted much like the modern chemical weapon called napalm.

Greek fire in small clay vessels could also be thrown like a hand grenade. It set fire to everything it touched and even burned underwater.

HEAVEN ON EARTH?

Constantine knew that a shared faith could help to unify his subjects. Christianity, now the dominant religion of the Roman Empire, permeated all aspects of Byzantine life. The Byzantines believed that Jesus Christ was the Son of God and the spiritual savior of humankind. They accepted Christ's teachings, which emphasized God's infinite mercy and love. They looked forward to an afterlife where, if they proved worthy, they would be united with God and Jesus in heaven. Those who disregarded church doctrine would suffer the fires of hell.

The Byzantine government was an autocracy. In theory, the emperor maintained complete control over all branches of government. He was considered God's counterpart, whose mission was to establish the "heavenly kingdom" on Earth. If an individual managed to take the throne, it meant that God was on his side. In some cases, people related by blood established ruling dynasties, but ambitious individuals of humble origins also seized power. Despite the advantages of that position, many Byzantine emperors died gruesome deaths—some were stabbed, strangled, beheaded, or blinded when public opinion turned against them. These revolts were seen as evidence of God's displeasure. Some of the approximately ninety men and a few women who ruled the Byzantine Empire were unqualified for the job; some were brutal and depraved. However, many truly effective rulers served the empire well and improved the lives of their subjects.

THE AGE OF JUSTINIAN AND THEODORA

The man who would become one of Byzantium's most successful rulers had an instinct for surrounding himself with the right people. The nephew of the emperor Justin, Justinian soon became indispensible to his uncle. People noticed his sharp intellect, remarkable energy, and determination. Justinian also found the perfect woman to marry. Beautiful and intelligent, Theodora began her life as the daughter of a circus performer. By the time she met Justinian, she had worked as a comedic actress and burlesque dancer. Apparently it was love at first sight. Byzantine law stated that actresses, who often worked as prostitutes, could not marry persons of high rank, so Justinian pressured Justin to change the law. Justinian and Theodora had some religious disagreements, but they remained completely devoted to each other throughout their married life. After his uncle's death, Justinian succeeded Justin to the throne, and Theodora became his empress and co-ruler of the empire.

Mosaics gracing the Basilica of St. Vitale in Ravenna, Italy, show the empress Theodora—robed in royal purple—with her attendants. She gazes across the church into her husband's eyes.

THE JUSTINIAN CODE

One of Justinian's greatest accomplishments was modernizing the Byzantine legal system. Over time, the Roman Empire had a developed a huge and cumbersome system of laws. As one of his first acts as emperor, Justinian hired a brilliant lawyer named Tribonian to simplify and clarify the legal system, eliminating outdated laws. The new legal system, called the Justinian Code, also introduced progressive new legislation. In accordance with Christian ideals of aiding the poor and powerless, Justinian established laws to help slaves and people suffering from debt. Theodora encouraged her husband to include laws that improved conditions for women.

WOMEN IN BYZANTINE SOCIETY

Byzantine women enjoyed a remarkable degree of power and influence in comparison to their lowly status in Roman life, Islamic culture, and in early medieval Europe. Byzantine culture placed a high value on education, and beginning at age five both boys and girls learned to read and write. However, most girls went on to learn household skills and were considered ready for marriage at age twelve or thirteen. Some wealthy Byzantine women did acquire an excellent classical education. Low-born individuals with energy and ambition could rise in society: the empress Theodora, for example, began her life as a circus performer.

Domestic violence afflicted many women in Roman society. In Byzantium, in part due to the teachings of Christianity, domestic abuse was frowned upon. Other advances won by

continued on next page

continued from previous page

Byzantine women included the right to divorce and to own some property. Women went on religious pilgrimages, commissioned art and buildings, and wrote historical accounts. They also shared in the highest levels of political power and ruled jointly with their husbands (as did Theodora) and as sole rulers themselves, such as the empresses Irene (reigned 797–802) and Zoë (reigned 1028–50). Women were pictured in the icons and mosaics of Constantinople much earlier than they were in western Europe.

THE NIKA REVOLT

Hippodromes were the sports arenas of their day. Male citizens from all levels of society would crowd in to these huge oval stadiums to watch chariot racing, political rallies, and sometimes a public execution. The hippodrome in Constantinople, completed by Constantine, was the largest in the world. Professional teams named for colors organized the events, which included entertainments such as boxing matches, exotic animals, and gymnastics. During Justinian's reign (527–65), the Blues and the Greens had become the dominant factions or "demes," with people swearing allegiance to one or the other. The demes eventually took on a political role, with one side chanting its support for a particular policy or shouting its disapproval of another.

Once displayed above the Hippodrome in Constantinople before it was taken by the Venetians, this sculpture depicts a *quadriga*, the four-horse team that pulled a carriage used for chariot racing.

In 532, the two rival factions found themselves united in anger against the emperor. Justinian had imposed steep taxes to finance his efforts to reconquer lost imperial territories. He had also restricted the privileges of both the Blue and Green factions. At a large gathering in the Hippodrome, the crowd roared *"Nika, nika!"* (Greek for "conquer"), calling for the emperor's removal. The imperial entourage scurried back to the palace via a secret passage from the stadium, and Justinian considered boarding a ship and fleeing the city. According to Procopius, a historian of the time, Theodora stood her ground. She told her husband that staying and facing death was preferable to giving up power. Justinian pulled himself together, and his imperial guards devised a brutal but effective solution to the crisis: they blocked the stadium exits and sent in soldiers to slaughter the 50,000 rebels trapped inside. The citizens of Constantinople would not soon risk the emperor's wrath again.

THE SECRET HISTORY

Many of the firsthand accounts of sixth-century Byzantium have survived thanks to a historian named Procopius. A trusted member of the Byzantine establishment and a private secretary to the general Belisarius, Procopius witnessed many of the significant events of the Justinian age. Procopius's official reports glorify Justinian and describe his accomplishments in glowing terms. But Procopius had a secret: he was writing another account, one that claimed to expose Justinian and Theodora for the demons they were. His *Secret History* tells a story of tyranny and corruption, perpetuated by a villainous emperor and his bloodthirsty wife. Procopius also wrote unflattering descriptions of Belisarius and his unfaithful and scheming wife, Antonina. If these writings had been found during his lifetime, Procopius would have surely been accused of treason. A copy of *The Secret History* was discovered centuries later in the Vatican Library and published in 1623.

AN ARCHITECTURAL MARVEL

Another great casualty of the Nika Revolt was Constantinople's central cathedral, which was torched in the rioting. Almost before the smoke had cleared, Justinian embarked on plans to build a new church, the Hagia Sophia, one much larger and more beautiful than the original. He hired two visionary architects to draw up the plans. With the help of 10,000 workers, the construction proceeded at an astonishing pace. Byzantium's wealth adorned the building with gold and different-colored marble and precious

The exterior of the Hagia Sophia was dazzling in Justinian's day. The four pointed minarets surrounding the domed structure are Islamic architectural features, added after the Ottoman Turks seized Constantinople.

stones. Glittering mosaics featuring images of Jesus, Mary, and Christian saints graced the interior. Priceless religious relics, such as the nails used to crucify Christ, were displayed beyond the high altar. The structure's crowning achievement was a massive domed roof—the largest unsupported dome in the world. Little more than five years after construction first began, Justinian stepped through the great doors and gazed in awe at his marvelous creation. Now stripped of most of its adornments, the Hagia Sophia is still one of the architectural wonders of modern-day Istanbul.

GENERAL BELISARIUS

Justinian had an excellent general at his command named Belisarius. A brilliant military tactician (possibly the greatest Roman general since Julius Caesar), Belisarius had helped to suppress the Nika Revolt. Justinian sent Belisarius with his army to reconquer territory that had been lost to barbarians such as the Vandals in Africa, the Ostrogoths in Italy, the Visigoths in Spain, and the Franks in Gaul (now France). The general and his men helped restore Italy to Byzantine control, and reclaimed the conquered city of Rome for the Roman Empire. Belisarius accumulated a huge amount of personal wealth from the various lands he plundered. He became so popular with the Byzantines that Justinian worried he might try to take control, but Belisarius remained loyal to his emperor. The famous mosaics in the St. Vitale church in Ravenna, Italy, may include a portrait of the general standing at Emperor Justinian's right hand.

ICON OR IDOL?

The Byzantines revered their icons, beautifully painted images of saints. They believed an icon gave them a direct means of communing with a holy person. Such religious images were often kept in the home and became the object of private worship, especially for Byzantine women.

The popularity of these images made some people worry—did icons violate the Second Commandment, which says that the people must not worship false idols? Emperor Leo III (reigned 717–41) told his subjects that the Arabs had achieved victories against the empire because Muslims banned all religious images. Byzantine defeats were surely God's punishment for the people's violation of His word. Leo sent soldiers to destroy the most important icon in the

city, a giant gold figure of Christ near the Hagia Sophia, sparking riots that spread from the city to the countryside. But the iconoclastic (meaning "image destroying") emperor was determined to purge Byzantium of its icons. His son and successor, Constantine V (reigned 741–75), carried on his father's iconoclastic policies. Monks fled the monasteries and hid their precious icons where the imperial soldiers could not find them.

Byzantine icons, such as this 14th-century image of St. Anthony, gaze straight at the viewer, encouraging the worshiper to feel a direct connection with the divine.

IRENE AND THE ICONOCLASTIC CONTROVERSY

A power-hungry woman named Irene would help put an end to the first iconoclastic controversy in Byzantium and further weaken the empire. The winner of an empire-wide beauty contest, Irene was chosen as a bride for Constantine's son, Leo IV. She secretly planned to restore icons to veneration. Eventually, she would become the first woman to rule the Roman Empire, first as regent for her ten-year-old son Constantine VI, and later as empress (797–802). She purged all the iconoclasts from the army, crippling its power. She had her son beaten and imprisoned

in a dungeon, and then blinded so brutally that he died, clearing the way for her to become empress. Feared and hated by the populace, Irene was finally forced into exile, leaving the empire in ruins.

The controversy was not officially settled until 843, by the second empress Theodora, widow of the emperor Theophilos (reigned 829–42). In a decision called "The Triumph of Orthodoxy," the veneration of icons was formally declared a feature of orthodox belief.

One of the few Byzantine women to wield absolute power, Irene's ambition was only surpassed by her cruelty toward her son.

CHAPTER 3

A SECOND FLOWERING: THE MIDDLE BYZANTINE PERIOD (843–1204)

The second great age of Byzantium occurred during the rule of the so-called Macedonians, beginning in 867 with Basil I. An Armenian who murdered everyone who stood between him and the throne, Basil turned out to be a surprisingly good emperor. He rebuilt the Byzantine navy, and struck back against the encroaching Muslims when they were weak and disorganized, reclaiming lost imperial territories such as Cyprus, Dalmatia, and southern Italy.

Basil I, first ruler of the powerful Macedonian dynasty, presides over a court banquet. The writing below the image is in Greek.

THE MACEDONIAN ERA (867–1056)

Basil also funded a public works program to refurbish Constantinople, where churches, public buildings, and monuments had fallen into disrepair. The city was rebuilt and Basil erected a splendid new church called the Nea Ekklesia (the "new church"), decorated with glorious mosaics to celebrate his rule. A patriarch named Photius, head of the Byzantine church, helped inspire a cultural renaissance, reintroducing the Byzantines to classical Roman and Greek literature. Basil also embarked upon a project to translate the Justinian Code from Latin into Greek. He hated his son Leo (Leo VI, reigned 886–912), who would nonetheless complete his father's recodification of Roman law and preside over a remarkable period of peace and prosperity.

CURIOUS NAMES OF BYZANTINE RULERS

Eighty-eight different emperors held power during the thousand years of the Byzantine Empire, and many of those in ruling dynasties had the same first names. Epithets, or nicknames, helped to distinguish one from another. Only a few rulers, such as Constantine, Justinian I, and Theodosius I, were successful enough to be called "the Great." Others were known by more colorful titles, such as:

- Justinian II the Slit-Nosed (reigned 685–95)
- Constantine V the Dung-Named (reigned 741–75)

- Constantine VI the Blinded (reigned 780–97)
- Michael II the Stammerer (reigned 820–29)
- Michael III the Drunkard (reigned 842–67)
- Constantine VII the Purple-Born (reigned 913–59)
- John II the Beautiful (reigned 1118–43)
- Andronicus the Terrible (reigned 1183–85)
- Alexius V the Bushy-Eyebrowed (reigned in1204)

THE QUEEN OF ALL CITIES

At the peak of its glory, Constantinople must have been a sight to see. The Byzantine court was designed to mirror God's court in heaven. Church ceremonies and imperial rituals were solemn and majestic spectacles. The imperial palace featured banquet halls, beautiful gardens, and a swimming pool. Clad in garments dripping with gold, pearls, and jewels, the emperor sat in a lavishly decorated throne room. According to one famous account from the tenth century, a foreign dignitary requested an audience with the emperor, who received his visitor while seated in a golden throne. The dignitary bowed deeply before the emperor. When he looked up, he was astonished to see that the throne had risen nearly to the ceiling and the emperor now wore an even more glorious robe. The Byzantine court made quite an impression on foreigners, as it was intended to. They returned to their lands to spread tales of the wonders they had seen in the Queen of Cities.

A THIRD SEX

Another feature of the Byzantine court that impressed visitors was the presence and status of eunuchs (pronounced YOU-nicks). These castrated men were trusted to attend to the emperor and empress. Their high-pitched voices and smooth, hairless skin added an exotic quality to court ceremonies over which they presided. Some eunuchs were originally castrated slaves; some families castrated their youngest sons to help them gain positions at court or in the church. Eunuchs might also lead armies. Narses, a general under Justinian I, was a eunuch who completed the conquest of Italy during that emperor's reign.

THE LAST MACEDONIAN

Most of the greatest emperors of the Macedonian dynasty had no blood ties to the throne. They were generals who rose to power while claiming to protect the interests of the legitimate heirs. They strengthened the empire and thus helped stem the tide of Islam, which had taken or was taking hold in neighboring areas in southwest Asia, northern Africa, and Spain. Crowned at age two, Basil II (reigned 976–1025) was the last great Byzantine conqueror. He spent years waging a relentless war against the Bulgarians, culminating in the crushing defeat that earned him his nickname "the Bulgar Slayer." Basil had 1,500 Bulgarian captives blinded, leaving every hundredth man with a single eye to lead the ragged remnants of the army back to its devastated tsar. Bulgaria became part of the Byzantine Empire. Basil expanded the

The soldier-emperor Basil II (crowned, to right of cross) had no patience for the extravagances of court life, and preferred to eat the same food as his soldiers.

imperial territory more than any emperor since Heraclius (reigned 610–41). Unfortunately he left no heir or successor to secure his achievements.

TERRITORIAL DEFENDERS

The Romans knew well the logistical problems of defending a large empire. In the seventh century, the emperor Heraclius had organized the imperial provinces in Asia and Europe into "themes," districts where, in exchange for land, troops were permanently stationed under the command of a military governor. Soldiers settled in the themes as farmers, in order to establish a permanent civilian army.

Over time, the number of themes multiplied. By the end of the eleventh century, Byzantium was comprised of thirty-eight themes.

The system helped to create a strong army with ties to the land. As time went on, however, landowners evolved into a powerful aristocracy, living like princes, acquiring more and more land at the expense of small farmers. Basil II had abolished land privileges and established laws to protect the poor. After his death the wealthy worked to overturn those laws.

A COSTLY ALLIANCE

By the twelfth century, the northern Italian city of Venice had become an important commercial power. Venetians excelled at shipbuilding and naval warfare. They traded slaves (often prisoners of war) to the Muslim world for spices, jewels, and incense. The Byzantine emperor Alexius I (reigned 1081–1118) forged an alliance with the Venetians: in exchange for providing naval power to help fight the Normans (originally Vikings from Scandinavia), Venice would be granted special trading privileges. Venetian merchants would pay little or no taxes on trade goods. Unfortunately, these concessions severely weakened the Byzantine economy.

THE GREAT SCHISM

Christianity was the official religion of Byzantium, but the Byzantines sometimes disagreed about the details of their faith. People at all levels of society enjoyed vigorously debating theological questions. Sometimes these arguments flared into violence. One persistent question concerned the nature of Jesus Christ. The Council of Nicaea had attempted to settle this by introducing the notion of the Trinity, and the orthodox view insisted on Christ's dual nature as both fully divine and fully human. However, Christians in Palestine, Egypt, and Syria disagreed with this idea. They believed in a wholly divine Christ. These Monophysites (pronounced "ma-NA-fa-sites," meaning "one nature") drew the wrath of the Byzantine authorities, who persecuted them for their beliefs. During the history of the empire, conflicts recurred between orthodox believers and Monophysites. When the new religion of Islam began to spread through this region, some Monophysites rejected the orthodoxy of their Byzantine overlords and adopted the teachings of the prophet Muhammad.

Another religious disagreement concerned differences between the eastern and western versions of Christianity. During the Byzantine Empire, the Christian church had two seats on power. One of these was in Rome, under the authority of the pope. The supreme authority of the Orthodox church, based in Constantinople, was called the patriarch. The Eastern church officials did not want to submit to the pope's authority—they believed the Orthodox church should be independent of papal control. In the west, Latin was still the language of religion and scholarship. The church was aligned with western culture and shaped by the traditions of the western European people. Greek was the official language of the Byzantine Empire, and Orthodox Christianity reflected Greek traditions and was more eastern in character.

This disagreement about religious authority lasted for years and drove the two branches of the Christian church farther apart. Eventually, in 1054, the Western and Eastern churches formally split in two. This division became known as the Great Schism. Over the years, various Byzantine emperors tried to heal the rift but with no success. The schism between the two branches became even further entrenched during the events known as the Crusades.

WAGING WAR IN GOD'S NAME

By the end of the eleventh century, about two-thirds of Christendom had been conquered by the Muslims, including regions of Palestine, Syria, Egypt, and Anatolia. The Crusades were a series of military expeditions organized by western European Christians beginning in the eleventh century. The Crusaders set out to stop Muslim expansion and to take back control of formerly Christian territories in the Holy Land. They also hoped to aid Christians living in the East and to conquer pagan lands. Many of the participants believed that being a part of these "holy wars" would please God and cleanse them of their sins.

The Crusaders' route to the east took them directly through Constantinople. In 1148, Anna Comnena, daughter of the Byzantine emperor Alexius I and perhaps the first woman historian, wrote an eyewitness account of the arrival of the Crusaders during the First Crusade in 1095.

Banished to a convent by her brother to prevent her from taking power, Anna Comnena dictated an invaluable history of her father's reign, known as the *Alexiad*.

THE FOURTH CRUSADE

After the schism, many western Christians scorned the Eastern Orthodox Church. They regarded its members as Greek heretics rather than as fellow Christians. In 1202, Pope Innocent III launched a fourth Crusade, bound for the Holy Land in Egypt, to reclaim land lost to the Muslims. The city of Venice had an uneasy history with Constantinople. The doge (leader) of Venice, a man named Enrico Dandolo, promised to supply ships for the crusaders if they agreed to attack Constantinople first.

The city was ill prepared to withstand the assault, and for the first time in history its walls were breached by an enemy—in this case, one that worshiped the same god. When the crusaders beheld Constantinople, and the magnificent palaces, glittering churches, and manicured gardens behind it walls, they were stunned. Once they came to their senses, they utterly destroyed it, looting and burning the city for three solid days. Almost no person or sacred object was spared.

The Venetians grabbed many of the most precious artifacts and send them back to adorn their own churches and palaces. Today, above the entrance to St. Mark's Basilica in Venice, visitors can see replicas of four life-sized copper statues of horses stolen from the Hippodrome of Constantinople. (The originals can be viewed inside the church, protected from the weather.) In the aftermath, the Venetians gained control of all the capital city's trading ports.

When the pope learned of the city's desecration, he was

horrified. In the name of Christ, Christians had mercilessly slaughtered fellow Christians and destroyed the most beautiful city on Earth. Members of the Eastern Orthodoxy would never forget, or forgive.

An illustration from a French illuminated manuscript shows ships being loaded with supplies in preparation for the Fourth Crusade. This so-called "holy war" would leave Constantinople in ruins.

CHAPTER 4

THE LATE BYZANTINE PERIOD (1205–1453)

I n the aftermath of the Fourth Crusade, the crusaders established a feudal Crusader state on lands formerly controlled by the Byzantine Empire. They placed a Western emperor on the throne. Sometimes known as the Latin Occupation, this undistinguished period in Constantinople's history lasted from 1204 until 1261. During this time, the urban capital was in terrible shape. The former Queen of Cities was a scene of deserted streets and crumbling buildings. The Latin emperor Baldwin II was so desperate for funds that he had the lead stripped off the palace roof and sold. He also pawned the few religious relics that remained in the city.

THE LATIN OCCUPATION

On the other hand, Byzantine towns and villages in the countryside were surprisingly well off. Tax collection had ceased with the collapse of the imperial government, and private citizens had managed to retain their wealth.

Towns grew into cities with strong economies. Merchants came from the east and west to sell their goods at fairs held throughout the empire, displaying wares from Russia, India, Africa, and China. Culture flourished, with new developments in art, architecture, music, and literature.

The Byzantine city of Mystras in Greece was founded after the Crusades devastated Constantinople. It is the site of the 13th-century Church of Agioi Theodoroi, seen here, and other notable examples of Byzantine architecture. Mystras was named a UNESCO World Heritage site in 1989.

THE EMPIRE IN EXILE

Now centered in the city of Nicaea, the patriarch, head of the Orthodox Church, represented the last fragment of the Byzantine Empire. Refugees poured into the city along with wealth, and Nicaea grew stronger. But the Latin emperors in Constantinople seemed oblivious to the growing threat of a Byzantine resurgence. In 1242, a Mongol horde swept in to crush the Seljuk Turks, warrior tribes originally from central Asia, but Nicaea was miraculously spared. The Byzantines took this as a sign of divine favor, and it fueled their dream of recapturing

Constantinople. This dream would come to pass with the help of a young general named Michael Palaeologus.

CONSTANTINOPLE RECLAIMED

In the summer of 1261, a Nicaean army of just 800 soldiers marched toward Constantinople to find the city virtually undefended. An unlocked gate allowed a handful of men to sneak in and overwhelm the guards. When the army poured through the opened gate, the Latin emperor Baldwin II fled in terror. Within a few hours the capital had been recaptured. The incredible news reached Michael, camped in his tent 200 miles away.

The returning Byzantines found their once-magnificent city in ruins. After fifty-seven years, the place had been stripped of its riches and left to decay. Houses were charred and dilapidated, and the mighty Theodosian Walls were in disrepair. The returning Byzantine emperor, crowned Michael VIII on August 15, 1261, resolved to restore Constantinople to its former glory. Rebuilding began immediately to repair the city's churches and monasteries and to shore up its walls. Schools reopened. Advances were made in sciences such as physics, astronomy, and mathematics. Hospitals, with both male and female doctors, ministered to the population. Michael VIII ordered the creation of a glorious new mosaic to adorn the Hagia Sophia: an image of Christ, framed by the Virgin Mary and John the Baptist, portions of which survive to this day. Blacksmiths forged a mighty iron chain, which was stretched across the harbor to block enemy ships from entering.

Large areas of the golden mosaic commissioned by emperor Michael VIII were chipped away after the Ottoman Turks conquered Constantinople and converted the Hagia Sophia into a mosque.

The emperor also designed a new imperial flag, featuring a golden double-headed eagle with two crowns, one representing Nicaea and the other Constantinople. The eagle's watchful gaze looked simultaneously to the east and the west.

ONE EMPIRE, MANY ENEMIES

Located between Europe and Asia and approachable by both land and sea, Constantinople was surrounded by many enemies. They coveted the empire's riches and trade agreements, and were eager to seize its territories. The Normans who had settled in southern Italy and Sicily were hostile to eastern Christianity. The empire's western neighbors the Venetians would betray the empire many times. From the north in Central Asia came the barbarian hordes, including Goths, Huns, Avars, Slavs, Gepids, Bulgars, and Pechenegs. To the east, until the beginning of the seventh century, the powerful Persian Empire posed a constant threat. The superbly fortified city of Constantinople managed to withstand onslaughts from Arab Muslims in the seventh and the eighth centuries. The eleventh century brought roving bands of Seljuk Turks, who spread quickly over Iran and Iraq, looting Byzantine territories in Armenia. Finally, after threatening the Byzantine capital for a century, the Ottoman Turks dealt the empire its deathblow.

THE LAST BYZANTINE DYNASTY

Michael VIII was the first and most successful in a series of emperors related by blood who would control the Byzantine throne between 1259 and 1453—the longest lasting dynasty in the history of the Roman Empire. A fiercely intelligent man and a skillful diplomat, he succeeded in outmaneuvering many enemies over the years of his reign.

However, one decision he made enraged his subjects: Michael needed the Christian West on his side to repel the dangerous Charles of Anjou, the King of Sicily and Naples. He promised the pope, Gregory X, that the Orthodox Church would submit to papal authority. When Gregory died in 1276, Charles of Anjou managed to have a French cardinal elected pope, who excommunicated the Byzantine emperor. Branded a heretic by the Western Church and a traitor by the Eastern Church, after his death, Michael VIII was buried without ceremony in an unmarked grave.

Meanwhile, the Ottoman Turks—Turkish tribes from Anatolia that had united—were growing in power. The Turks and the Byzantines were longtime political rivals, yet Muslim Turks sought Christian Byzantine princesses as brides. Each culture influenced the other. As the Byzantine Empire shrank, the Turks gained ground. They had seized land in Anatolia and marched north into the Balkans (in eastern Europe), overtaking the Serbs, the Hungarians, and the Bulgars, and conquering most of Greece. Churches were converted into mosques, and Christian peasants began to renounce their beliefs and adopt the new religion of Islam.

Pope Gregory X (in power from 1271 to 1276) hoped to mend the schism dividing the church. Over time, the papal miter (ceremonial hat) would become taller and more tapered.

THE FINE ART OF DIPLOMACY

The Byzantine Empire managed to survive for over one thousand years by relying more on persuasion and cleverness than on military strength. Wars cost money and human lives. To avoid fighting them, the Byzantines strategically recruited allies, fooled threatening neighbors, and tricked potential enemies into attacking each other. When the Sicilian king Charles of Anjou posed a threat to the Byzantines, Emperor Michael VIII encouraged the Sicilians to rebel against him. When the Byzantines did resort to sending their own soldiers, they preferred military policies that contained rather than destroyed the enemy. They knew alliances could shift rapidly, and today's enemy might be tomorrow's ally.

Byzantine rulers sent trusted nobles and clerics on diplomatic missions to other countries. They stayed well informed about the lands they visited and supplied regular reports to the court in Constantinople. An organization called the "Bureau of the Barbarians" kept extensive written notes on Byzantium's allies and enemies. They knew the strengths and weaknesses of foreign peoples and which leaders could be bribed or intimidated. When foreign envoys came to see the emperor in his golden court, he made sure to dazzle them with the prospect of riches to be gained if they chose to aid the empire.

Christian missionaries represented another diplomatic strategy used by the Byzantines. One way of neutralizing an enemy was to convert him to Christianity. Two Byzantine monks journeyed to the Balkans and into

continued on next page

continued from previous page

Greece. They developed a Slavonic alphabet (later known as Cyrillic, which is still used today) to teach the illiterate Slavs to read and write and to give them access to the Bible. Missionaries also used music in the form of hymns and chants to help win people to their faith. Many Slavs and Bulgars adopted orthodox Christianity as their religion.

NATURAL DISASTERS

In the middle of the fourteenth century, what remained of Byzantium experienced a series of natural disasters. Most of Constantinople's population sickened and died in 1347 during an outbreak of the bubonic plague, known as the Black Death. Carried by fleas traveling on shipboard rats, the plague always struck port cities first. During the empire's long history, several epidemics of this disease had severely reduced the population, nearly killing the emperor Justinian I in 542.

Additionally, due to the seismic activity in the region, Constantinople suffered many earthquakes over the years. In 740, a quake split the massive dome of the Hagia Sophia. In 1354, a major earthquake struck the Thracian coastline and damaged the walls of the port in nearby Callipolis (now known as Gallipoli). Seizing the opportunity, the Ottoman Turks were able to take the city.

EMPIRE'S END

The Ottoman sultan, or ruler, Mehmet II came to power following the death of his father, Murad, in 1451. Mehmet was determined to take control of Constantinople, and to install himself there as "Caesar" of the Roman Empire. The Turks had a new weapon called "the imperial," a mighty cannon that could propel a 1,400-pound (635-kilogram) ball a mile (1.6 kilometers), smashing through stone walls that had managed to repel invaders for centuries. During nearly two months of bombardment, the Byzantines worked frantically each night to repair the city walls.

Ladders mounted on ships helped the Ottoman Turks storm the walls of Constantinople in 1453, while the remaining defenders of the city fought in vain to hold them off.

The massive chain continued to stretch across the water and block the entrance to the harbor. However, the Turks hauled their smaller ships over the hills and launched them in the harbor to begin an assault by water. A fleet of relief ships promised by the Venetians never arrived.

The Byzantines fought ferociously, but they were overpowered by the twenty-one-year-old sultan and his soldiers, who outnumbered them by more than 17 to 1. When Mehmet and his army broke through the walls of Constantinople on May 29, 1453, the remaining Byzantines didn't have a prayer. Turkish soldiers rampaged through the city, slaughtering and raping the remaining 50,000 inhabitants, and looting and burning the churches. Icons were smashed, and religious articles were desecrated.

The last Byzantine emperor, Constantine XI, fought and died anonymously with his people. He had shed his purple cloak, a symbol of his imperial status, and his body was never identified. Framed by two rulers named Constantine, a civilization that had survived for 1,123 years and 18 days had finally had been brought to an end.

Ultimately, the surviving Byzantines may have felt that domination by a Muslim power was preferable to rule by the Christian West. As some said, "Better the Sultan's turban than the Pope's miter." Whatever their differences, the Christian Byzantine Greeks and the Muslim Turks were not natural enemies. For the first half of the fifteenth century they had coexisted as neighbors and trading partners. Now Islam had triumphed, and the city of Constantinople would become the capital of the Ottoman Empire.

CHAPTER 5

THE LEGACY OF BYZANTIUM

For centuries after its fall, the Byzantine Empire had a terrible reputation. The eighteenth-century English historian Edward Gibbon wrote a monumental work called *The Decline and Fall of the Roman Empire*. In it, Gibbon casts the Byzantine Empire in a very negative light, describing it as "the most thoroughly base and despicable form that civilization has yet assumed." The adjective "Byzantine" has a negative connotation, meaning overly complicated and devious.

Recently, historians have begun to take a more balanced view. They have a richer understanding of Byzantine culture and an appreciation of the many ways it shaped world history. Scholars now emphasize the key roles the eastern Roman Empire played in the formation of Europe and the evolution of the Middle East. Some even credit the Byzantines with saving Western Civilization.

THE LITTLE GOLDEN FORK

In 1005, a Byzantine aristocrat named Maria Argyropoulina astonished Venetian society and changed people's eating habits forever. At a banquet, rather than eating with her hands, as everyone else did at the time, she used a small, golden, two-pronged fork to spear her food and lift it to her mouth. Witnesses were amazed, and many imitated the practice. Soon forks became luxury objects.

The refinement of Byzantine culture was also reflected in the fact that many bachelors in the West wanted to marry Byzantine brides. These unions were considered

prestigious, and the women brought rich dowries with them, including silken clothes, religious icons, and elaborate gold jewelry. However, some Western clerics condemned Byzantine customs as a bad influence on their culture. This view of the Byzantines as a decadent and corrupt civilization would color historians' attitudes toward the empire for centuries.

Gold-and-enamel earrings such as these once adorned the earlobes of a wealthy Byzantine woman. Examples of finely wrought Byzantine jewelry have survived to be admired in museums today.

SAILING TO BYZANTIUM

The imperial court in Byzantium amazed visiting dignitaries, who described perfumed fountains, jeweled mechanical birds that sang in metalwork trees, and mechanical lions that roared. Slavic ambassadors in the tenth century returned home with tales of unimaginable splendors, saying, "We knew not whether we were in Heaven or Earth."

The British travel writer Robert Byron (1905–41) famously described the Byzantine Empire as a "triple fusion," possessing a Roman body, a Greek mind, and a mystic soul. The word "Byzantium" has always evoked a lost world of luxury and mystery. It cast a spell over the Irish poet William Butler Yeats (1865–1939). In "Sailing to Byzantium," Yeats wrote of his desire to be gathered into the "artifice of eternity," the immortal realm of art, and to escape the mortal world where flesh decays:

...

Once out of nature I shall never take
My bodily form from any natural thing,
But such a form as Grecian goldsmiths make
Of hammered gold and gold enamelling
To keep a drowsy Emperor awake;
Or set upon a golden bough to sing
To lords and ladies of Byzantium
Of what is past, or passing, or to come.

PRESERVING THE CLASSICS

After the collapse of the Western Roman Empire, the European provinces once under imperial control were left ungoverned. People had to reorganize themselves under local systems of leadership. They grouped in villages around fortified castles. Feudal systems evolved, where peasants farmed the land in exchange for the protection of a nobleman. During these so-called "Dark Ages," most western Europeans could not write their own names.

During its long lifespan, the Byzantine Empire also suffered periods of cultural decline, where literacy rates dropped. Yet Byzantine scholars always managed to resume their studies of science, literature, medicine, art, and engineering. They worked hard to preserve classical texts of Greek and Roman literature and philosophy, including works by Plato and Aristotle. Byzantine scribes copied approximately 40,000 of the 55,000 ancient Greek texts that survive today. They carried these texts west with them into Europe after the collapse of the empire, where they became the basis for the traditions of Western learning.

THE ISLAMIC GOLDEN AGE

Contacts with the Byzantine Empire also helped stimulate learning in the Muslim world. The Islamic Golden Age, an economic, cultural, and scientific flourishing, lasted from the eighth to the thirteenth century. The city of Baghdad held an enormous library called the House of Wisdom, where many classical Greek and Roman texts obtained from the Byzantines were translated into Arabic. Much of the science, philosophy, and mathematics that came from the Muslim world drew upon the work of the ancient Greeks.

THE SHIELD OF THE WEST

The walls of Constantinople managed to stall the advance of Islam into Europe for eight hundred years. During the seventh century, the Byzantines held back the Arab Muslims. Later, they blocked the Turks from advancing. Forced to take the long way around by land rather than traveling more quickly by sea, Muslim powers were delayed in extending their influence into this part of the world. This allowed the West time to develop its own distinct cultures and to strengthen its Christian traditions.

NEW CENTERS OF ORTHODOXY

When Mehmet the Conqueror began to repopulate Constantinople under the flag of Islam, he made room for Byzantine Christians as well. A monk was appointed to the post of patriarch. Not all churches were converted into mosques. Kept alive, Orthodox Christianity preserved its traditions and rituals. Eventually known as the Eastern Orthodox Church, it gave rise to a branch of Christian Orthodoxy based in Moscow, Russia. Though violently suppressed under Communist rule, today the Orthodox Church of Russia has multitudes of followers. In Greece, the flag of the Eastern Orthodox Church still features the two-headed Byzantine eagle. The monastery of Mount

Athos (Holy Mountain) in northern Greece, established in 963, remains one of the most important centers of Christian Orthodoxy. The modern-day Eastern Orthodox Church is now the second largest Christian church in the world.

LAW AND DIPLOMACY

Advances in law and diplomacy from the Byzantine period are still in practice today. The emperor Justinian I reformed the laws of ancient Rome, preserving the empire's principles of reason and justice. Legal codes in much of Europe and Latin America are based on the Justinian Code.

Beset by enemies on all sides, the Byzantines also refined the practice of diplomacy to an art form. They gathered intelligence on foreign powers and kept extensive written records. Avoiding warfare whenever possible, they manipulated their opponents through intricate diplomatic designs. The Byzantine practice of actively interfering in the events of other territories has now become commonplace in today's foreign policy.

This illustration from an illuminated copy of the Justinian Code shows a dying man attended by two monks administering last rites.

INFLUENTIAL IMAGES

During the last two centuries of its existence, the Byzantine Empire produced some of its finest artwork. Artists developed a more naturalistic style, using techniques from ancient Greek and Roman art to express Christian themes. The beauty of Byzantine mosaics, frescoes, and religious icons influenced important painters of the early Italian Renaissance such as Giotto and Duccio. Today, major museum exhibitions of Byzantine treasures, icons, and illuminated manuscripts collected from around the world have inspired a new appreciation for this brilliant and complex society.

HEAVENLY ARTS

Byzantine art is religious art. While Byzantine artists created beautiful everyday objects, such as jewelry and textiles, their dominant subject matter was religious, taken from the Old and New Testaments. Byzantine artists did not strive to express themselves or create something unique. Their role was to translate the beliefs of the Orthodox Church into the language of art. Therefore, very few Byzantine artists are known by name. Their portraits of saints are traditional—doing something strikingly original would have been considered heretical. Whereas ancient Greek art celebrated the natural human form, Byzantine artists were dedicated to the supernatural, immortal realms.

continued on next page

continued from previous page

Similarly, most surviving Byzantine architecture is religious. Byzantine rulers lavished money on churches, creating bigger structures with more mosaics and high windows to bring in more sunlight. The dome, echoing heaven's arch, was an important architectural motif. Besides the Hagia Sophia in Istanbul, one of the most splendid examples of Byzantine architectural style is St. Mark's Basilica in Venice, Italy.

The exuberant façade of St. Mark's Basilica reflects Byzantine influences as well as the Venetian sunshine. Venice's main attraction houses many of the looted treasures of Byzantium.

SEEING THE PAST IN THE PRESENT

The Byzantines were a fascinating and sophisticated people who look back at us across the centuries with the same level gazes as the figures in their icons. They passionately debated many of the same theological and political questions that continue to ignite conflicts around the globe. Learning about their history opens a window onto the world of the past and the present: understanding the many challenges they faced and all they managed to accomplish can help us gain perspective on where we stand today. If not for the Byzantine Empire, the world as we know it would not exist. We can forgive the Byzantines for sometimes believing that they were the most interesting people in the room. They probably were.

TIMELINE

c. 658 BCE Byzantium is founded by Greeks.

312 CE Emperor Constantine embraces Christianity.

324 Constantine chooses Byzantium as the new capital of the Roman Empire.

325 The Council of Nicaea defines Orthodox Christian faith.

330 Byzantium is renamed Constantinople in honor of the Emperor Constantine. The city is dedicated as the new capital of the Roman Empire.

392 Pagan religions are banned.

413–39 Theodosius II builds new city walls.

476 Rome falls to the Ostrogoths. The Roman Empire in the West ends.

527–65 Justinian I reigns over the Byzantine Empire.

529 The Justinian Code is compiled.

532 The Nika Revolt prompts rioting in Constantinople.

533 General Belisarius takes back North Africa from the Vandals and Sicily and Italy from the Ostrogoths.

527 The Hagia Sophia is completed.

610–41 Heraclius rules the empire.

674–78 The First Siege of Constantinople by the Arab Muslims takes place.

717–18 The Second Siege of Constantinople by the Arab Muslims takes places.

717–41 Leo III rules the empire.

726–80; 813–42 The era known as the Iconoclast Period takes place.

751 Byzantines lose control of northern Italy to the Lombards.

800 Charlemagne is crowned Roman emperor in the West.

842 Icon veneration is restored after the death of Theophilis in what is known as "The Triumph of Orthodoxy."

867–86 Basil I, founder of the Macedonian Dynasty (867–1056), rules the empire.

976–1025 Basil II (Basil the Bulgar Slayer) rules the empire.

TIMELINE

1054 The Great Schism occurs.

1071 Seljuk Turks defeat the Byzantine army in Anatolia.

1081–1118 Alexius I Comnenus rules the empire.

1082 The Byzantines make trade agreements with the Venetians.

1098 The First Crusade stops at Constantinople and then moves on to take Jerusalem.

1118–43 John II the Beautiful, son of Alexius I, rules the empire.

1202–04 The Fourth Crusade takes place and results in the sacking of Constantinople.

1204–61 Latin emperors rule Constantinople.

1261 Michael VIII Palaeologus, emperor of Nicaea, restores Byzantine rule.

1409 The last attempt to achieve unity between Roman Catholic and Greek Orthodox churches occurs with the Council of Florence.

1448 Constantine XI becomes emperor.

1453 Constantinople falls to the Ottoman Turks, led by Mehmet II. The Byzantine Empire ends.

GLOSSARY

autocracy A government in which one person has unlimited power.

barbarian To the Byzantines, a foreigner, specifically someone not Greek or Roman.

Byzantium The part of the world under the control of the Byzantine Empire; also the original name of Constantinople.

Caesar A title taken by Roman emperors after Augustus.

Christendom The part of the world where Christianity prevails.

Crusades A series of "holy wars" initiated by the Catholic Church, waged between the eleventh and thirteenth centuries, to recapture cities from Muslim control.

desecrate To purposefully destroy, damage, or insult a sacred place or object.

diplomacy The practice of conducting peaceful negotiations between nations without resorting to violence.

ecumenical Universal; refers to worldwide Christian unity or cooperation.

eunuch A man or boy whose testes or external genitals have been removed.

excommunicate To deprive a person of the rights of church membership.

heretic One who dissents from an accepted belief or doctrine.

icon A religious image, often featuring a saint or a religious subject, painted on a wooden panel.

iconoclast Meaning "image destroyer"; a person who opposes the veneration of religious icons.

Islam The religious faith of Muslims, which includes belief in a single god (Allah) and his prophet Muhammad.

mosaic A surface decoration made by inlaying small pieces of colored material to form a picture or design.

Monophysitism The belief that Jesus Christ has one divine nature and is not both human and divine.

GLOSSARY

Muslim A follower of Islam.

Orthodox Conforming to established religious doctrine.

pagan A follower of a polytheistic religion, such as was practiced in ancie nt Greece and Rome.

relic An object that is esteemed or venerated because of its association with a saint or a religious martyr.

schism A formal division or separation from a church or a religious body.

siege A military blockade of a city or fortified place to force it to surrender.

theme A district where a number of farmer-soldiers were stationed under the control of a military governor.

Dumbarton Oaks Byzantine Collection
1703 32nd Street, NW
Washington, DC 20007
(202) 339-6401
Website: http://www.doaks.org/museum
Dumbarton Oaks is home to one of the world's finest collections of
   artifacts from the Byzantine Empire, including icons, jewelry, coins,
   textiles, ceramics, and everyday objects such as eating utensils. It
   is also the site of the Byzantine Institute of America.

The Metropolitan Museum of Art 1000 Fifth Avenue (at 82nd Street)
New York, NY 10028
(212) 535-7710
Website: http://www.metmuseum.org
The Met's vast collection includes the Mary and Michael Jaharis
   Galleries for Byzantine Art and the Medieval Europe Gallery with
   numerous examples of Byzantine art. Also on display is the Jaharis
   Byzantine Lectionary, a rare 12th-century manuscript.

Royal Ontario Museum
100 Queen's Park
Toronto, ON M5S 2C6
Canada
 (416) 586-8000
Website: http://www.rom.on.ca
The Royal Ontario Museum is home to the Joey and Toby Tanenbaum
   Gallery of Byzantium, which houses the largest collections of
   Byzantine art in Canada, and the Joey and Toby Tanenbaum Gallery
   of Rome and the Near East.

Russian Orthodox Cathedral of the Transfiguration of Our Lord
228 N 12th Street
Brooklyn, NY 11211
(718) 387-1064
Website: http://www.roct.org
This Orthodox cathedral in Greenpoint-Williamsburg dates from

1922, and is the only example of its kind of Byzantine Revival architecture in New York and perhaps the United States. It is listed in the National Register of Historic Places, and all visitors are welcome.

St. Kosmas Aitolos Greek Orthodox Monastery
55 Caledon King Townline South
Bolton, ON L7E 5R7
Canada
(905) 859-2474
Website: http://www.saintkosmasaitolosgomonastery.org
Established in 1993, the St. Kosmas Aitolos Greek Orthodox Monastery is a religious organization within the Greek Orthodox Metropolis of Toronto, Canada. St. Kosmas Monastery follows the Cenobitic way of monastic life (meaning "common way of life") consisting of common work, common meals, and common rest periods as practiced by ancient Christians. Visitors to the monastery are welcome.

The Walters Art Museum
600 North Charles Street
Baltimore, MA 21201
(410) 547-9000
https://www.thewalters.org
Internationally renowned for its collection of art spanning the third millennium BCE to the early twentieth century, the Walters Art Museum is a public museum founded in 1934. The museum houses an extensive collection of early Byzantine art.

WEBSITES

Because of the changing nature of Internet links, Rosen Publishing has developed an online list of websites related to the subject of this book. This site is updated regularly. Please use this link to access this list:
http://www.rosenlinks.com/RFE/byzan

FOR FURTHER READING

Andersen, Zachary. *The Fall of Rome and the Rise of Constantinople.* New York, NY: Cavendish Square, 2015.

Angold, Michael. *The Fall of Constantinople to the Ottomans: Context and Consequences.* Oxford, England: Taylor & Francis, 2014.

Brownworth, Lars. *Lost to the West: The Forgotten Byzantine Empire That Rescued Western Civilization.* New York, NY: Three Rivers Press, 2010.

Evans, Helen C. *The Glory of Byzantium: Art and Culture of the Middle Byzantine Era, A.D. 843–1261.* New York, NY: Metropolitan Museum of Art, 2013.

Harris, Jonathan. *The Lost World of Byzantium.* New Haven ,CT: Yale University Press, 2015.

Herrin, Judith. *Byzantium: The Surprising Life of a Medieval Empire.* Princeton, NJ: Princeton University Press, 2007.

Kallen, Stuart A. *Life During the Roman Empire.* San Diego, CA: ReferencePoint Press, 2013.

Komnene, Anna, and Peter Frankopan, ed. *The Alexiad.* New York, NY: Penguin Classics, 2009.

Mathisen, Ralph W. *Ancient Mediterranean Civilizations: From Prehistory to 640 CE.* New York, NY: Oxford University Press, 2014.

McKinley, Harald P. *Persia, the Rise of Islam, and the Holy Roman Empire.* New York, NY: Cavendish Square, 2016.

Procopius. *The Secret History.* New York, NY: Penguin Classics, 2007.

Rosser, John H. *Historical Dictionary of Byzantium.* Lanham, MD: Scarecrow Press, 2011.

Stathakopoulos, Dionysios. *A Short History of the Byzantine Empire.* London, England: I.B. Taurus & Company, 2014.

VanVoorst, Jennifer Fretland. *The Byzantine Empire.* Mankato, MN: Capstone Press, 2012.

Vasiliev, Alexander. *History of the Byzantine Empire.* Madison, WI: University of Wisconsin Press, 2012.

BIBLIOGRAPHY

Antonucci, Michael. "War by Other Means: The Legacy of Byzantium." *History Today*, vol. 43, issue 2, February 1993 (http://www.historytoday.com/michael-antonucci/war-other-means-legacy-byzantium).

Brownworth, Lars. *Lost to the West: The Forgotten Byzantine Empire That Rescued Western Civilization*. New York: Crown Publishers, 2009.

Brownworth, Lars. "12 Byzantine Emperors: The History of the Byzantine Empire." Podcast. Retrieved November 30, 2015 (http://12byzantinerulers.com).

Dash, Mike. "Blue versus Green: Rocking the Byzantine Empire." *Smithsonian*, March 2, 2012 (http://www.smithsonianmag.com/history/blue-versus-green-rocking-the-byzantine-empire-113325928/?no-ist).

Harrell, Eben. "A New Exhibit Uncovers the Secrets of Byzantium." *Time*, October 24, 2008 (http://content.time.com/time/arts/article/0,8599,1853629,00.html).

Harris, Jonathan. *The End of Byzantium*. New Haven, CT: Yale University Press, 2010.

Herrin, Judith. *Byzantium: The Surprising Life of a Medieval Empire*. Princeton,NJ: Princeton University Press, 2007.

Luttwak, Edward N. *The Grand Strategy of the Byzantine Empire*. Cambridge, MA: The Belknap Press, 2009.

Marston, Elsa. *The Byzantine Empire*. Tarrytown, NY: Benchmark Books, 2003.

Norwich, John Julius. *Byzantium: The Early Centuries*. New York, NY, Alfred A Knopf, 2007.

Rosen, William. *Justinian's Flea: The First Great Plague and the End of the Roman Empire*. New York, NY: Penguin Books, 2007.

Treadgold, Warren. *A Concise History of Byzantium*. New York, NY: Palgrave, 2001.

Wells, Colin. *Sailing from Byzantium. How a Lost Empire Shaped the World*. New York, NY, Delacorte Press, 2006.

INDEX

INDEX

Gregory X, 39

H

Hagia Sophia, 21–22, 23
Heraclius, 29
heretics, 33, 40, 51
hippodrome, 18

I

iconoclasm, 23, 24
icons, 23, 24, 46, 51
imperial flag, 38
Irene, 24
Islamic Golden Age, 48–49

J

Jews, 11
Justinian I, 15–22, 50
Justinian Code, 17–18, 22, 26

L

Latin Occupation, 35–36
law and diplomacy, 17, 41–42, 50
Leo III, 23
Leo IV, 23

M

Macedonian era, 26, 28–29
Mehmet II, 43–44
Michael VIII, 37, 39
military, 22, 29–30
missionaries, 41–42
Monophysites, 31
mosaics, 18, 22, 26, 51–52
Muslims, 23, 25, 32, 39, 48–49

N

natural disasters, 42
Nea Ekklesia (the "new church), 26

Nicaea, 36
Nicene Creed, 12
Nika Revolt, 18–20, 21, 22

O

Ottoman Turks, 39, 40, 42, 43–44

P

pagans, 11
Palaeologus, Michael, 37
patriarch, 31, 36, 49
Persian Empire, 39
Photius, 26
Procopius, 19, 20

R

Roman Empire, 6–10
Rome, 7, 9–10, 22

S

Secret History, 20
Seljuk Turks, 36, 39
Slavs, 39, 42

T

themes, 29–30
Theodora, 15–16, 19–20
Theodosius I, 11
Theodosius II, 13
trade, 9, 30, 38
"Triumph of Orthodoxy," 24

V

Venetians, 30, 34, 39, 44
Venice, 30, 33–34

W

women's rights, 17–18

ABOUT THE AUTHOR

Monique Vescia has written dozens of nonfiction books, on subjects ranging from animal behavior and fashion to historical reenactments and poetry. Researching the world of the past has helped her to better understand the complexities of the present. She lives in Seattle with her husband and fellow writer, Don Rauf, and their teenage son. The first item on her travel bucket list is the city of Istanbul.

PHOTO CREDITS